A NOTE TO PARENTS ABOUT LYING

It's a real dilemma: How can children be taught to be truthful when a large portion of their lives is immersed in fiction? Also, how can children be motivated to tell the truth when doing so might result in them being punished?

The purpose of this book is to help children understand the difference between fantasizing, being mistaken, and purposely lying. In addition, it teaches children the importance of telling the truth.

Reading and discussing this book with your child will inspire him or her to be truthful. It can also teach your child the appropriate way to behave if he or she has been dishonest.

Since the fear of being punished keeps most children from being truthful about their misbehavior, it is important to remove the threat of punishment from any request for the truth. When a suspected misbehavior occurs, assure your child that there will be no punishment if he or she tells the truth. After your child has confessed to a wrongdoing, make clear to your child that although his misbehavior is unacceptable, you're proud of him for having told the truth. Then discuss with your child how he thinks he should behave in the future. Once a mutually agreed upon pattern has been established, make certain you and your child follow through with it.

This book belongs to:

Grad 4

HOPE '81

Grad 2 level

LUMLEY

Published by Scholastic Inc.
90 Old Sherman Turnpike, Danbury, CT 06816.

SCHOLASTIC and associated logos are trademarks and/or
registered trademarks of Scholastic Inc.

ISBN 0-7172-8576-6

First Scholastic Printing, September 2005

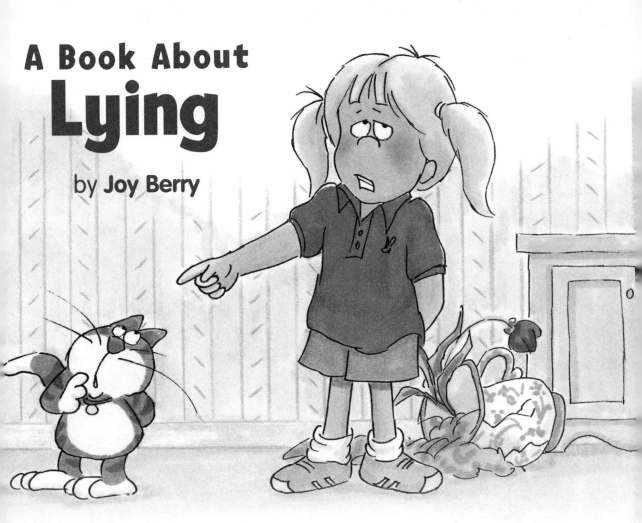

A Book About
Lying

by Joy Berry

SCHOLASTIC INC.

New York   Toronto   London   Auckland   Sydney
Mexico City   New Delhi   Hong Kong   Buenos Aires

This book is about Katie.

Reading about Katie can help you understand and deal with **lying**.

Sometimes you might make up a story and tell it to other people for fun.

An untrue story that is told for fun is called a *fantasy*.

It is OK to tell a fantasy. But it is important to remember that the fantasy is not true. It is also important to make sure that others know it is not true.

Sometimes you might say something you think is true. Then later you might discover that what you said is not true.

When you do not know that what you are saying is untrue, you are making a mistake.

It is OK to make mistakes because no one is perfect. Everyone makes mistakes.

Sometimes you might purposely tell someone something that is not true. When you do this:

- You are not telling a fantasy.
- You are not making a mistake.
- You are lying.

Lying is trying to make someone believe something that is not true. It is *deceiving* or *fooling* someone on purpose.

Lying is not a good thing to do. When you lie:

- You disappoint other people.
- You cause people to wonder if you ever tell the truth.
- You cause people to stop trusting you.

People who do not trust you might not believe you when you are telling the truth.

This is not good. There are times when you need to have people believe you.

So, you should not lie.

There are many ways to tell lies. You can tell lies *with your actions.*

You might cause someone to believe something that is not true by acting a certain way. You are lying when you do this.

You can tell lies *with your silence.*

You might cause someone to believe something that is not true by not saying anything. You are lying when you do this.

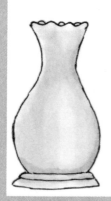

You can tell lies *with your words.*

You might cause someone to believe
something by saying things that are untrue.
You are lying when you do this.

People usually find out when you lie to them.

Do not try to cover up a lie by telling more lies. This will only make things worse.

Tell the truth if you have lied.

Admit that you have lied. Say "I lied to you."
This will begin to make things better.

Say that you are sorry if you have lied.

Do everything you can do to show you are truly sorry you lied.

Then do not tell any more lies.

If you want people to believe and trust you, you must not lie to them.